Advent 2011

Call Him God's Son

ALEX JOYNER

An Advent Study Based on the Revised Common Lectionary

Abingdon Press / Nashville

CALL HIM GOD'S SON
by Alex Joyner
An Advent Study Based on the Revised Common Lectionary
Copyright © 2011 by Abingdon Press

ISBN-13: 9781426716225

Manufactured in the United States of America

11 12 13 14 15 16 17 18 19 20—10 9 8 7 6 5 4 3 2 1

Contents

Introduction

I always start Advent with the best of intentions. I know the dangers of the season: the tendency toward excess, the marketing of excess, and the social pressure to do everything to excess. It can be measured in advertisements, credit card bills, hours spent, and pounds added on my body. It may also be measured by a certain emptiness of spirit that can creep up on me when I least expect it. Poignant memories of times past and loved ones lost, a longing for something more lasting and meaningful. It is a dangerous season.

So I try to ready myself. New Year's resolutions are nothing compared to the Advent resolutions I make: resolutions not to spend too much; to focus on relationships rather than retail; to incorporate silence and simplicity into my celebrations; and, most importantly, a determination to let Jesus be at the center of it all. However, I find that the season overwhelms these good intentions.

Study books can only go so far in keeping me on track. They cannot be an end to themselves. However, if they can send me back to the rich biblical texts of the season and help me encounter those texts in new and powerful ways, well, maybe I will worry less about the resolutions and live more fully with the desire for God.

Ultimately this is what Advent is about—nurturing the restless desire for God that is the hallmark of true humanity. When all else fails in our lives, when we reach our end, the thirst and hunger for God will remain. Jesus reveals this as he comes into the longing world.

In this study we explore what it means that Jesus is God's Son. We explore the creative tension of living in a world caught between what is and what is promised to be. We look at the healing capacity of hope to sustain us in times of trouble. We try on incarnation in its divine and human forms, and we look to Mary as a figure who shows us how to make space for God.

My hope for this study is that it may be an aid to you in staying close to what is right in front of you. If *Emmanuel* means that God is with us, then we should not have to have a lot of apparatuses to experience God's presence. Resolutions too often are one more level of distraction. I pray this book can be a window to help you see what has been there all along.

As I landed at an airport on a recent flight, the cabin attendant misspoke as she welcomed us to the arrival city. "Be careful as you open the overhead bins," she said, "as your longings may have shifted during the flight." I smiled, but I know that is just what good journeys do. They change us, and our longings may shift. I invite you to an Advent journey that can do just that. May you receive the gift of longings redirected toward God.

Living in Creative Tension

Scriptures for Advent: The First Sunday
Isaiah 64:1-9
1 Corinthians 1:3-9
Mark 13:24-37

The opening Scripture passages of the Advent season arrive like a shock to the system. We anticipate peace and light. Instead we get a hard edge and dark warnings. We are tempted to rush past these biblical texts. Yes, there are uncomfortable things that need to be said and done if the world is going to see God's transformation; but we would rather hear of it in the strains of "Joy to the World" inviting the earth to "receive her king." However, Isaiah prepared the way with rags and leaves; and Jesus talked about suffering, sacrilege, and a darkened sun.

Tension is the watchword of the early days of Advent. We find tension between the long-told story of Jesus' birth and the long-anticipated coming of Christ again. We find tension between the promise of a restored and redeemed world and the pain that accompanies such transformation. Then we find the tension of living in Christian community as it waits. It is a tense time.

This season is also a creative time. Somewhere, gestating in the gathering storm, something new is preparing for birth. Nurtured on the vision of a God-filled world, sustained by the knowledge of God's past faithfulness, and consumed by the fire of God's love for the earth, a new incarnation is coming to this old world. It promises to come to remake us as well.

Where does God choose to make an appearance? Does God discard all that has gone before and start again? No, the Strength of Israel remains with the covenant established long before with Abraham and his descendants. The Hope of the Nations enters again into the conflicted story of Israel, a people now long past the days of their former glory. Here God says, "I will do a new thing."

The story of Jesus' coming into the world is full of drama and challenge. It is a human story with cosmic implications. We may feel we know this story all too well. We might want to bypass the discomfort; but as we settle into these texts, we feel the invitation to a life of creative tension.

A RAG, A LEAF, AND A LUMP OF CLAY
ISAIAH 64:1-9

The lights go up in the storefronts. Along the main streets of the town, workers labor from bucket trucks to place Christmas trees formed from tinsel on the light poles. Christmas music, from the warm tones of Perry Como to the majesty of large choirs, plays over loudspeakers as we walk through the shopping mall. Everything around us tells us that Christmas is coming, so why do so many of us feel a certain distance from the season, perhaps even a certain dread? Christmas is coming, and we are far from ready. It is not just that our preparations are not finished; our souls are not ready.

I have a chunk of concrete on a shelf in my office. The concrete is a piece of a church. I got it when I went with a mission team to Piedmont, Alabama, in the summer of 1994. We went because of what had happened on March 27 of that year. On that day, Palm Sunday, about 140 people had gathered for the 11 A.M. service at Goshen United Methodist Church. The children were doing a musical program, and the procession had just begun.

At just that moment, a huge tornado was cutting a half-mile swath across the county. When it hit the church, it lifted the roof off and then crashed it and the walls down on top of the people inside. Twenty people died. More than 40 people died in three states during that storm, but it was the church that got our attention.

One of the children who died was Hannah, the four-year-old daughter of Kelly Clem, pastor of Goshen Church. "This might shake people's faith for a long time," she said. "I think that is normal, but having your faith shaken is not the same as losing it."[1] So the next Sunday, with the cameras from national television networks there and her eyes still blackened from the collapse of the roof, Kelly Clem led her church in an Easter sunrise service in the parking lot next to the ruins of the church. Those of us watching shuddered. We professed belief in God. We knew that life triumphed even in the midst of death, but could we have done what Kelly did?

When our team arrived a few weeks later to work on houses that were being rebuilt in the wake of the storms, we traveled with Kelly's mother. Kelly's husband, Dale, is also a United Methodist minister; and he was the one who took us on a tour of where the church had stood. At the time, it was just a collection of broken bricks and concrete. Dale talked about a cross that had survived the tornado. Everything else in the church had signs of damage, but the cross that was being used for the Palm Sunday service had survived untouched. That was his sign of hope in the midst of all the inexplicable suffering. Yes, there was death and there was rubble; but there was still a cross that witnessed to something beyond death. That is when I picked up my piece of Goshen Church that still sits in my office.

As Advent begins, we hardly know where to look for God. We take joy in the bright lights and tinsel, but we know that they are not the answer to the deep longing of our souls for a new day and for God. The chunk of concrete speaks powerfully to the desire for God to come into the darkness.

The prophet Isaiah emphasized the absence of God in this passage from Chapter 64. Speaking for the people who were waiting on a God to deliver them from exile, Isaiah called for God to tear open the heavens and come down with earthquakes to make the earth tremble. However, Isaiah suspected that God was absent because of the people's sin. A people living without God are no people at all.

So how do you describe such a people? "We have all become like one who is unclean, / and all our righteous deeds are like a filthy cloth. / We all fade like a leaf, / and our iniquities, like the wind, take us away" (verse 6). A filthy cloth. A leaf being blown in the wind. There is not much to recommend a people who are far from God. Maybe it is a little like having a tornado come through and take away everything upon which you have built your hope.

Isaiah used one more image: "We are the clay," he said to God, "and you are our potter; / we are all the work of your hand" (verse 8). It is an old biblical image. You could say it is at the beginning in the opening chapters of Genesis. After all, what was Adam before God blew the breath of life into him? Earth. Dirt. Clay. This pottery image goes way back.

We can imagine potters who work so carefully on a formless ball of clay. Can you see her? She is bent over the wheel, forearms covered in clay, hands immersed in mud. Then, almost magically, the clay begins to take shape in her hands, becoming when it is finished, what she knows it was always meant to be. They are connected. Without the potter, the clay is a lump. With the potter, the clay becomes the bowl, the pitcher, or the cup.

This is the image Isaiah used to describe us before God. If we are going to see God, if we are going to be redeemed from the situations that threaten to take away our hope, if we are going to be changed and remade, if the world is going to become better instead of worse, we must give ourselves to God like formless clay before the potter. For Christmas to come, we give ourselves to God to be remade into the people God desires us to be.

We often say that the amazing thing about Christmas is that God comes to us in human form. God becomes human in order to save us and this world from the effects of sin and destruction. We might also say that one of the other effects of the Incarnation is that we also have the opportunity to become human, to become what God intends us to be.

God has created human beings in such a way that we are born with the capacity to be transformed. I do not know what sorts of sins a platypus gets into, but I suspect that they do not need to be transformed and remade. We, however, not only can be transformed, but we must be transformed. God gives us everything we need in order to be transformed. We are not condemned to accept the world as it is or to accept ourselves as we are. We can know hope, possibility, and change even when everything around us seems to deny it.

This is why in the midst of the Holocaust, even when their homes had been taken, their families separated, their loved ones killed, their neighborhoods and synagogues destroyed, Jewish culture survived. People sang and made music in the death camps. In the Warsaw ghetto, people wrote articles for newspapers. People told stories to their children because they knew that eventually even the Nazis would pass and transformation would come.

So when Isaiah says that we are like filthy rags, like leaves in the wind, we can say, "Yes, but we are also clay awaiting transformation. God can take us and remake us. A new day is coming; and it belongs, not to the worst of us, but to God." How much do our lives reflect this understanding? Does Advent say for us that we are proclaiming this new day that is coming; or does it say that we are just going to do more of the same, only this time with more lights and glitter?

What symbols speak to you most powerfully about the message of Advent? What parts of your life do you need to offer up for transformation?

A COMMUNITY FOUNDED IN BROKENNESS
1 CORINTHIANS 1:3-9

A celebrant stands at the table and takes a cup filled with the crimson fruit of grapes. The words are as ancient as the apostle Paul and as mysterious as the day he wrote them down: "The cup of blessing that we bless, is it not a sharing in the blood of Christ?" Similar words accompany the breaking of a loaf: "The bread that we break, is it not a sharing in the body of Christ?" (1 Corinthians 10:16).

I have been that celebrant on many occasions. Sometimes I look over the cup at a group of people who seem filled with a unity of spirit that feels heavenly. Sometimes, between the fractured halves of the upraised bread, I see a divided and fractious community with multiple unresolved conflicts. The table around which the church gathers for Communion is where it all comes together. This is where our most essential story is told. This is where we meet Christ in the sharing of a meal. This is where we draw together as a body to meet one another in the intimate act of eating. As in any group that eats together regularly, when we get together at the table, we are forced to confront the tensions between us.

Paul invites us to share in the blood and body of Christ, a reminder that we find out who God is through Jesus' suffering and death in this world. The word that we translate as "sharing" in 1 Corinthians 10:16 is also the word that Paul used to describe the relationship of the community to Christ in 1 Corinthians 1:9. *Koinonia* is the word in Greek; and it has the connotation of close connection, social bonding, and generosity. Paul reminds us that "God is faithful; by him you were called into the [*koinonia*] of his Son, Jesus Christ."

To be brought into relationship with Christ is to become part of a society of others who share Christ's name. The result can be tumultuous. Just ask the Corinthian Christians. After this lofty theological affirmation in the opening verses of the book, Paul goes on to address the mundane and messy problems that have arisen in the community. Sharing one another's lives had opened up a world of sexual misconduct, envy, pride, jockeying for status, and more. Without reorientation to their first love, the community would find itself in no different position than any other group in the city.

I often imagine that the early days of the Methodist movement in North America were times of greater cooperation and concord than we see in many congregations today. As a young movement drawing people into close-knit small groups where they could hold one another accountable for their growth in holiness, surely they experienced a level of harmony that we can only imagine. Not so. Deep relationships were formed; but perhaps because of the depth of their relationships, the Methodists were sometimes a raucous bunch.

On the Eastern Shore of Virginia, one of the places where Methodism took early and vibrant root, the stories of circuit riders are dotted with stories of conflict. Thomas Smith was one of the early preachers traveling in this area around 1800. He talked about conducting preaching series to great effect, despite the fistfights that broke out among the congregants.[2] The outpouring of the Spirit did not eliminate the real tensions of human community.

What will tame these tensions? Perhaps the recognition of a greater tension focused on the coming of Christ. Paul mentioned Jesus Christ throughout these opening verses of the first letter to the Corinthians. He authorized his position with the community by referring to himself as an apostle of Jesus Christ (verse 1). He reminded the community that they had been "sanctified," set apart to be made holy by Christ Jesus (verse 2). They did not exist on their own but were part of a church that included "all who call on the name of our Lord Jesus Christ" (verse 2). Paul blessed them in the name of Jesus (verse 3), he gave thanks for the grace that God had given them in Jesus (verse 4). He celebrated how the witness to Christ had been strengthened among them (verse 6).

Finally, Paul discussed why Jesus is so important: He is coming back. The revelation begun in Jesus will continue. A day will come when the wrongs of this world will be made right, and Christ will be made known as the one who shows that God's justice is meant for everyone. As they waited for that day, the Corinthian Christians were to remember their gifts and remember that they had been drawn into a new relationship in Christ.

Paul was trying to reorient the Corinthians around their center. The anchor of their identity and their hope was in Jesus. They had been remade in him. Like the spokes of a wheel that move from the rim to a central point, as they approached the center, they would find that they were also drawing closer to other believers. In that coming together, they could become distracted, or they could maintain their direction and be part of a dramatically different kind of community.

Dietrich Bonhoeffer, in his treatment of Christian community, *Life Together,* says that the fact "that we are brethren only through Jesus Christ is of immeasurable significance." It means that we relate to one another, not because of any quality that might have drawn us to one another but because we share what Christ has done in and for us. "I have community with others and I shall continue to have it only through Jesus Christ. The more genuine and the deeper our community becomes, the more will everything else between us recede, the more clearly and purely will Jesus Christ and his work become the one and only thing that is vital between us."[3]

Taken in isolation, the words of thanksgiving that Paul offers in this passage obscure the real work that he was attempting to do. He wanted the church to be strengthened and ready. He knew that in order to be strengthened and ready, they would have to come to terms with who they were as a body. If they did, perhaps they would see how Christ was coming again in the visible growth of true community.

What conflicts are you involved in that could be remade by opening yourself to Christ? What symbol could you carry with you (for example, a cross or a small stone) to remind you that you wait for Jesus Christ?

REMAINING IN PLACE
MARK 13:24-37

It is often the case in the United States that the first Sunday in Advent comes three days PT (post-turkey). Thanksgiving is a long weekend of excess for many of us. The great meal. The shopping binges that are encouraged by advertisements for the cheerily-named Black Friday. The explosion of twinkling lights and music promising winter wonderlands and joy to the world. Then comes Sunday, and the message is not about any of this. The Jesus of Mark 13:24-37 is not cooing from a manger but warning of hard times to come and a day of final judgment.

Mark 13 is sometimes called "The Little Apocalypse" because it contains a collection of Jesus' sayings about the end of time. These verses give us a taste of the whole. The signs of Christ's coming are dramatic: The sun will be darkened. The moon will not shine in the night sky, and the stars will fall from the heavens. Then Christ will come in power and glory to gather in the chosen.

Naturally enough, it inspires a question for us as for the disciples in Jesus' audience: "When will this be?" (verse 4). Jesus had given his followers all sorts of premonitions of what was to happen to them. There would be suffering and pain for the chosen people of God. An appalling sacrilege would be set up in a high and holy place. False

messiahs would lead others astray. "When you see these things," Jesus says, "you know that he is near" (verse 29).

All of these things did happen in the lifetime of most of Jesus' listeners. The new Christians did suffer. Profane rites were performed in the Jerusalem Temple. False messiahs plagued the early church. However, what Jesus said is troubling. Even though he would not give dates and he said that no one—not even the Son—knows when that day and hour will be (verse 32), still he said that "this generation will not pass away until all these things have taken place" (verse 30). The signs of which Jesus spoke did take place; yet we are left to wonder why the promised event itself, the advent of Christ in the clouds, has yet to come.

Be ready. That is the message of this passage. Wouldn't it be easier to be watchful and waiting if we knew that within our lifetime the fulfillment of all things would happen? However, it must not have been easy at all.

Jesus told a parable about a man leaving his house and giving a charge to the doorkeeper to be awake when he returned (verses 34-37). Jesus' hearers would have understood themselves to be the doorkeepers. Yet Peter, James, and John, three disciples who were especially close to him, were given the same command by Jesus only one chapter later. As he went to pray in the garden of Gethsemane,

Jesus told them to "remain here, and keep awake" (14:34). What happened? Three times he returned to find the disciples sleeping!

If they could not manage it, how shall we? Two thousand years on, we are not so vigilant. Christ's return does not seem so immanent. If the challenge for the Corinthian Christians was to deal with the tensions of their community, it seems that one of our challenges is to live in a time without tension. On the face of it that seems ridiculous to say. No tensions? Forget the stress of the season. What about the economy? the wars? the climate? Surely all of these indicate tension.

In contrast to Jesus' words, though, it does seem that time has stretched out. The end, even one brought about by nuclear holocaust, does not feel quite so near. The tension of living at the tail-end of history has dissipated. In a world that has lost any sense that something great and meaningful is at stake in the passing of time, what are Christians called to do?

In monastic communities, particularly those in the Benedictine tradition, there are certain vows that individuals take as they enter the community. One of these is a vow of *stabilitas*. The Latin word is visible in the word *stability*, but it suggests much more than not moving. In the monastic tradition, the vow was a commitment to remain in a place, in a community, until death. Some modern intentional Christian communities have renewed the old vow with the understanding that new members of the community are pledging to live within it as if it will be the place where they die.

Either notion of *stabilitas* is a countercultural challenge to a contemporary society that discourages individuals from staying put or staying in relationship when times get tough. We are all about moving on. Remaining on the scene challenges us to live in creative tension with the world. We have the opportunity to see through the situation before us to a larger, deeper reality.

According to the Benedictine writer Joan Chittister, "Stability says that where I am is where God is for me. More than that, stability teaches that whatever the depth of the dullness or the difficulties around me, I can, if I will simply stay still enough of heart, find God there in the midst of them."[4]

Staying awake, being ready, and keeping watch will not be fruitful if we accept the diminished expectations of the world around us. If we concede that there is nothing vital on the horizon and no transformation coming, then we do not inhabit the promise of Christ's coming. Advent invites us to *stabilitas*. It claims this time and space and invests it with far more depth and wonder than the world gives it. Observing Advent means vowing to remain in this space until the illusions fade away and God's radical reign is revealed in the coming Christ.

If you lived out of the expectation that Christ was coming again, what would change about the way you live day to day? In what difficult places or relationships are you being challenged to stay in place to find God?

[1] From "Piedmont Journal," by Rick Bragg in *The New York Times* (April 3, 1994).
[2] From *History of Franktown United Methodist Church*, by Randolph Walker (Franktown United Methodist Church, 1994); page 8.
[3] From *Life Together*, by Dietrich Bonhoeffer, trans. by John W. Doberstein (HarperCollins, 1954); pages 25-26.
[4] From *Wisdom Distilled From the Daily: Living the Rule of St. Benedict Today*, by Joan Chittester (HarperCollins, 1990); page 151.

Living With Hope

Scriptures for Advent:
The Second Sunday
Isaiah 40:1-11
2 Peter 3:8-15a
Mark 1:1-8

When he entered the National Football League as a running back for the Minnesota Vikings, Adrian Peterson made an immediate impact. As a rookie he piled up yardage and ran through defenses with seeming ease. I remember that one commentator remarked on the way that Peterson squared his shoulders toward the goal line and ran straight toward it, not wasting time with lots of cuts from side to side. He remarked that it was like Peterson was already in the end zone in his mind and his body was just fighting to catch up, and that this was what made him so effective.

Advent invites us into a similar kind of altered consciousness. It comes in a season of distractions in the midst of a life full of distractions. It catches us when we are preoccupied with many things. Students are working through exams. Businesses are preparing for end-of-the-year tallies. Shoppers are preparing for Christmas.

Those living on the margins are struggling to survive. Many people are dealing with feelings of loss and grief that become especially acute around the holidays. It is easy to think that these realities constitute the whole of our lives. We lose sight of where we are headed.

The Scriptures for this second week of Advent focus on hope for a reality that has been promised and that is coming into being. The texts call us to look deeply into the world around us for unexpected signs of God's coming reign.

Isaiah compares human life to grass but then places our lives in the greater context of God's unfailing promise. Fire and cataclysmic destruction take the foreground in the Second Letter of Peter, but the deeper promise is of a new heaven and a new earth. John the Baptizer cuts a striking pose as the harbinger of good news in the Gospel of Mark.

The Scripture readings prompt us to live out of a different reality formed by our hope for a new day instead of our preoccupations. What if the world is filled with the presence of God, and we just do not know it? What if, despite all the pundits' predictions and all the settled wisdom, God is coming to make all things new? What if our hope is already in the realm of God's reign, and we are just running to catch up to it?

HOPING AND LOVING DEEPLY
ISAIAH 40:1-11

Louie Zamperini had no cause for hope. He was drifting across the Pacific Ocean on a canvas and rubber raft with two fellow survivors. They were airmen in World War II, flying missions out of Oahu. One day in 1943, they were on a rescue mission when their B-24 spun out of control and crashed in the ocean, killing all but the three who survived. For over a month they floated across the waters, hoping for land and rescue.

In her book *Unbroken: A World War II Story of Survival, Resilience, and Redemption*, Lauren Hillenbrand brings to life the story of Louie and these men. Zamperini had been a track star who went to the 1936 Olympics. Many thought he would be the one to break the four-minute mile, but all of his training had gone to prepare him for something different.

Sharks circled the raft, and the men eventually had only albatross and random fish to eat. They grew thinner. The experience was taking its toll, but there was a marked difference in how each man reacted. Louie and Phil, the plane's pilot, maintained a conviction that they were going to survive, while their fellow airman, Mac, slipped into despair. Louie discovered that he could pray; and "Phil was a deeply religious man, carrying a faith instilled in him by his parents. . . . Phil never spoke of his faith, but as he sang hymns over the ocean, conjuring up a protective God, perhaps rescue felt closer, despair more distant."[1]

The men drifted on. Mac eventually died en route, in part because he did not share the hope of his companions and lost the will to go on. Louie and Phil were rescued by Japanese forces and went on to endure even greater hardships in POW camps. Their hope did not fail them, though. They survived that experience as well.

One mark of being human is to live with hope, to look forward to what God is doing in the world, and to see the miraculous things that are already at work because of the love we know in Jesus Christ. If we can only see what is wrong with the world, then we have missed the Advent vision that something is ultimately right with the universe because God has come to redeem it.

The Isaiah passage from last week's study gives us strange

images of Advent: the filthy rag and the dried-up leaf. This passage gives us images that are more gentle. Remember that Isaiah was trying to bring good news to the people of Israel in exile. They had been carted off to a foreign land. They had lost everything they held as sacred—the land, the Temple, and their king in the line of David. Jerusalem, the Holy City, had been destroyed. They were being oppressed by the great Babylonian Empire.

Isaiah's first words here were "comfort, O comfort my people, / says your God. / Speak tenderly to Jerusalem, / and cry to her / that she has served her term, / that her penalty is paid, / that she has received from the LORD's hand / double for all her sins" (40:1-2). This God was going to redeem them from their suffering.

Isaiah offered a vision of a grand highway stretching across the desert to take the people back home. They would not have to go home the long way following the course of rivers. They would not have to worry about mountains and valleys impeding their travel. They would not have to worry about potholes and detours. This road would go straight through the desert to take them home. This road was the highway of God. When the nations saw this caravan going home, they would know that Israel's God was a mighty God.

Then Isaiah followed up this message of hope with a strange phrase that does not, at first, sound like hope: "All people are grass" (verse 6). They do not have any more staying power than a flower in a field—here today and gone tomorrow. "Surely the people are grass" (verse 7). Was he saying that we are hopeless creatures who wither into insignificance? Was he saying that ultimately nothing matters because ultimately we fade away? Was he saying that God gets a kick out of our humiliation, or was he saying something much deeper and much more hope-full?

The next verse says, "The grass withers, the flower fades; / but the word of our God will stand forever" (verse 8). Our lives have meaning, purpose, direction, and hope because they are connected to God's story. If we are going home, it is not because of anything we have done. It is because of what God will do for us and with us and in spite of us for no good reason except God's pure love.

Hope for Christians is built on the notion that our gifts and talents are only of use when they are placed in the service of something larger. We are constantly bumping up against that "something larger," which can make us feel small and insignificant. However, the response Isaiah called for was not to hang our heads in despair or to approach our lives with downcast eyes.

In essence, Isaiah said, "Look at yourself. See that you are limited and that your power to sustain yourself will ultimately fail, but also see yourself in the light of the one who is to come. See that your story does not end with fading flower and withering grass. See that your hope is not placed in your ability to achieve liberation and success. See that your worth is not determined by what you can earn monetarily or by what power you can exercise over others. See that suffering and oppression are not what God intends for the creation. See that you are like grass and flowers and that God loves you for what you are!"

What does hope look like for Christians? It looks like Jesus. It looks like people who put themselves in the footsteps of Jesus and try to model their lives after him.

For me, it looks like one of my first colleagues in ministry, Kathleen Baskin-Ball. In the summer of 1989, we went into ministry in the inner city of Dallas, Texas. I was beginning my seminary internship as the youth coordinator for a community center. She was going to start a new congregation in the abandoned church next door. Neither of us knew what we were doing or what to expect. Both of us were Anglo Americans just learning Spanish, and we were working in a Latino neighborhood. Kathleen was single at the time, only about 30 years old. She was idealistic and charismatic, and she loved everybody.

Our paths crossed a lot that year. We were working with many of the same youth, and they formed the nucleus of her new church community. I remember the meeting in her house when we started talking about a name for the new congregation: Nueva Esperanza—New Hope United Methodist Church.

I remember one cold night near Christmas when the two of us were the guitarists as we walked through the streets of West Dallas with a borrowed donkey. We sang door-to-door in a celebration of *Las Posadas,* a Mexican tradition that remembers the journey of Mary and Joseph trying to find a room in Bethlehem.

Kathleen was never satisfied with doing ministry from a distance. She got a house near the church. She said the experience opened her eyes to realities of life that she could not have seen before that. It was a difficult period for her; but she was convinced, as she said later, that "when it's not convenient, when it costs us and we still take the time to listen to another's heart and we love deeply, hope emerges,"[2] she said.

Hope did emerge through Kathleen's ministry. Youth went to college who would never have gone. People came to know a powerful God in an impoverished part of the city. Five years after she came to an empty church building, 130 members were part of the Nueva Esperanza congregation.

Kathleen went on to serve two other churches and was a well-respected leader in the greater church when she was diagnosed with cancer. The prognosis was not good. She continued to preach and to serve even though her voice was often weakened and hoarse. Four days before she died, she was receiving people in her home against everyone's best judgment; but she was not going to stop loving deeply. So she hugged her visitors, comforting them when they had come to comfort her.

The witness that people like Kathleen offer reminds us that our hope is not built on everything going right. We do not look forward to the future because it promises to be Easy Street. We look forward to the future because God is already there. When our winter eyes lead us to count only our losses and wounds, God says, "Comfort, comfort my people."

When has hope sustained you through a period of crisis? How can confessing our limitations lead us to greater freedom to be human?

THE BEST IS YET TO COME
2 PETER 3:8-15A

The earth has been destroyed so many times at the cineplex that it is a wonder we are still here. Surely with all the imagined threats to human existence, one of them must have come to be by now. Movies point to nuclear holocaust, aliens, pandemics, zombies, natural disasters, or the end of the Mayan calendar as potential agents of mass destruction. We line up at the box office to imagine all the apocalyptic possibilities.

The Second Letter of Peter certainly offers its own share of images of global destruction. We find all-consuming fire, horrific noises, melting stars, and blazes that consume the earth—all for our Advent enjoyment! Were the early Christians who read this letter just as hooked on stories of their imminent demise as we seem to be?

What is it that we contemplate when our thoughts turn apocalyptic? The term has come to be synonymous with ultimate, cosmic catastrophe; but *apocalypse* means "revelation." (The Greek title of the last book of the Bible can be rendered as "The Apocalypse.") When the ancient church was waiting on the return of Christ, they looked forward to the uncovering of the world in its reality. Jesus' return would definitively show what was true and essential about the world. So Peter's readers desired the coming of the end of the world because then its end, or purpose, would be revealed.

The thing about end-of-the-world movies, though, is that they rarely deliver on their promise. The world does not end. People usually survive. No matter the gravity of the disaster, someone makes it through and life continues. That is what we go to see, isn't it? We want to understand how anything makes it when the world falls apart. We want a cathartic story of hope and maybe even love among the ruins. Though the crises we face in daily life may not qualify as world-ending, they can seem intractable, insurmountable, or impossible to survive. We want to be saved from them.

Second Peter 3:15 says, "Regard the patience of our Lord as salvation." In paraphrase, that was how the author imagined the frustration of his audience. "You look for the great signs and wonders in the sky. You look for a powerful display of God's might and judgment on the evils of this age. You want Jesus to make good on his promise to return soon. It seems that God has forgotten. It seems that time marches on without God's presence. Perhaps the Second Coming is all a ruse." This paraphrase might also describe our frustration 20 centuries later.

God measures time differently than we do, the letter says. "A thousand ages, in [God's] sight, are like an evening gone," to quote the Isaac Watts hymn "O God, Our Help in Ages Past." From the perspective of eternity, the brokenness and fallen state of this world find its place within the vision of a restored and redeemed creation that is yet to be revealed. This does not mean that the time we live in is insignificant. It does not mean that the pains and struggles we experience are not worthy of attention. God is doing something in this "slack" time, according to this letter. In this time when we are waiting on God, God is waiting on us. God is waiting for the world to see what is going on, and God is not willing any to be lost.

So what does that mean for the impatient Christians of yesterday and today who long for some kind of sorting out? It means a particular kind of lifestyle. It means dedication to high moral standards and living in peace with one another. It means being a distinctive people who live with a particular understanding of time.

I can remember driving through the grasslands of southern Oklahoma some 20 years ago. The towns in the Red River valley came along infrequently; and many, with their lonely, vacant downtown buildings, seemed to speak of better days long since past. One weathered settlement had a metal sign at the town's edge. The sign was bent and pockmarked with pellets from a shotgun blast—not a promising gateway to the community. On the sign, however, was a message clearly visible beneath the damage, which read, "The best is yet to come."

That is the motto for all Advent people. As verse 13 reminded its original readers and reminds us, what we hope for is not destruction. Violent upheavals of the created order may come, but they are not the source of our hope. "We wait for new heavens and a new earth, where righteousness is at home." Until that day comes, we live as people who already have our feet planted in a space where the best has come.

Where are the spaces in your life and your community where you would put a sign that says, "The best is yet to come"? If you stood in that space and took that sign seriously, how would you view and act upon its promise?

FACING THE TRUTH
MARK 1:1-8

Mark's Gospel begins with the activity of John the Baptizer in the wilderness. What is striking is why he appears at the beginning of Mark's Gospel. The book begins by saying that it is a story of the good news of Jesus Christ, Son of God. Conditioned by Christmas stories told from childhood, many Christians would be expecting the next line to say something about babies, mangers, or shepherds. Instead, Mark, the most habitually impatient of the Gospels, launches us into the desert with John so that we can get ready for a fully adult Jesus who will appear only eight verses later.

What is the rush? Well, a climactic struggle was about to begin. Ancient prophecies were being dusted off for a new age. Isaiah's vision of a voice crying, "Prepare the way" was finding new meaning. Whereas before the voice proclaimed a new way *through* the wilderness to bring the exiles home, now the *voice* was in the wilderness and the way of the Lord was taking a path through human hearts. Getting ready had never been so personal.

In Matthew's Gospel, Jesus asked his followers about their attraction to John the Baptizer. "What did you go out into the wilderness to look at . . . Someone dressed in soft robes? Look, those who wear soft robes are in royal palaces. What then did you go out to see? A prophet? Yes, I tell you, and more than a prophet" (Matthew 11:7-9). John certainly looked the part of a prophet. We might find his choice in clothing and diet a tad strange. (Camel hair? Locusts? Really?)

However, at a gathering of Israel's prophets, John would have fit right in. After all, Ezekiel lay on his side for months on end as a witness. Jeremiah wandered around naked at one point. However, John appearing in the desert in this way was not the most striking thing about him. He was a charismatic figure, and people came from all the surrounding regions to hear what he had to say. Expectations for a messiah, an anointed savior, were running high. It seemed to many that this prophet in the wilderness might be the one they were waiting for. The rugged desert-dweller was surely a good candidate for the role.

John, however, was certain that he was not the one. "The one who is more powerful than I is coming after me," he proclaimed (Mark 1:7). Mark makes clear that Jesus was the one who had the power. From the time that the heavens broke apart at his baptism and the Spirit descended on him, Jesus was stalking the land, rebuking the death-dealing forces that would distort God's intentions for the world. Demons fled when he spoke to them. He silenced unclean spirits; and when his opponents accused him of acting under the authority of Satan, Jesus made clear that evil was not his master but his enemy. "No one can enter a strong man's house and plunder his property without first tying up the strong man" (3:27). That is what Jesus is about—binding up evil.

So how did John ask the people to get ready? By going down into the river Jordan to be baptized. Their ancestors had crossed the Jordan centuries before in order to receive the land promised to them by God. The location would have reminded them of God's covenant, and the act of baptism would have recalled the ritual washings required to make the priests and the people clean. It was an act with a physical effect but a spiritual intent. John told them it was a baptism of "repentance for the forgiveness of sins" (1:4).

Forgiveness was required to help them leave behind their past. Repentance was about turning around and identifying themselves with the God who was coming into the world for their redemption.

One of the roles of the prophets was to clarify what was at stake in the midst of the mundane decisions people were called upon to make. Whether they were speaking to kings considering national alliances, to elders about their judgments at the city gate, or to individuals about their regard for the poor, prophets tried to make clear what was at stake. They revealed God's interest and presented stark images of God's desires. After a prophet spoke, you could not pretend that your daily decisions were of no consequence.

In his "Letter From the Birmingham Jail," Martin Luther King, Jr. wrote to a group of well-meaning clergy about his vision of what was happening in the city. King had been jailed for activism in support of civil rights for African Americans and had been criticized by the clergy for pushing too hard. They were supportive of his ends but found fault with the means, feeling that he might alienate others by creating tension in the community.

King responded prophetically. He noted that he did not create the tension. The tension was inherent in the unjust system that enforced racial segregation and relegated black citizens to second-class status. What King and his fellow activists were doing was exposing what was going on and demanding that all citizens—no matter their race—take a stance on the side of justice. There was no room for ignorance, innocence, or inaction once the offense was clear.

John had a similar impatience with lifestyles that cover over the fundamental disease that afflicts us. The reality of sin and injustice operates in contradiction with the presence of God in the world. To pretend that there is no conflict is not acceptable any longer. What is crooked will have to be made straight.

I recognize my aversion to facing the uncomfortable truths about the world and about myself. Acknowledging the truth entails confrontation with what must be done to change the situation, so I try to ignore the fact that I have neighbors just down the road with substandard housing and no indoor plumbing. I distract myself from addressing the barriers that keep me from calling my difficult relatives. I hold my tongue when I feel my friend is going astray rather than risking a real relationship and saying what God leads me to say. I pull back from the discipline required to maintain my health.

What was it that those people of the Judean countryside went out to see in the wilderness? If John was compelling enough to get them to overcome their own aversions to truth, then perhaps he was the beginning of the good news. It takes an extraordinary figure to get us to confront reality and then to point us away from despair.

The real message of the Baptizer is that even after the lid is blown off of the world's injustice and inhumanity, even after our own internal failures are exposed, God is on the way. The strength to change has entered the world. The one who is stronger than John is coming, and no power on earth can resist this one.

What truth about yourself have you been resisting? Who has acted like John in your life, helping you see the reality of your life as God sees it?

---

[1] From *Unbroken: A World War II Story of Survival, Resilience, and Redemption,* by Lauren Hillenbrand (Random House, 2010); pages 147-48.
[2] From "Longing for More: Hope," by Kathleen Baskin-Ball, sermon (Suncreek United Methodist Church, Allen, Texas, December 9, 2007); *suncreekumc.org/worship/sermons.asp.*

Incarnation for All

Scriptures for Advent:
The Third Sunday
Isaiah 61:1-4, 8-11
1 Thessalonians 5:16-24
John 1:6-8, 19-28

The German theologian and church leader Dietrich Bonhoeffer, who was executed in a Nazi death camp, once wrote that God's coming in human form was a dramatic statement, not only about who God was but also about who we are. "Human beings become human because God became human, but human beings do not become God. They could not and cannot bring about that change in their form, but God himself changes his form into human form, so that human beings—though not becoming God—can become human."[1]

In the passages for this week's study, the promises of previous weeks are taking shape in a particular way. Isaiah talked about a restored community that embodies God's presence in the world. Writing to the Thessalonian Christians as they awaited Christ's imminent return, Paul invited them to live with joy in their present circumstances. John the Baptizer confronted the representatives of the Jerusalem religious leaders as they came out to interrogate him. He only increased their sense of unease by talking about the one who was among them already. Each passage emphasizes the ways God is coming into the world and the ways God's people incarnate God's love and presence through their life together.

Bonhoeffer reminds us that Incarnation is not only God's gift in Jesus, but it is God's promise for all. We are not divine, but we can be fully human because of what Jesus has done. That has consequences, not only for us but for the whole world. It means that the reign we wait for is emerging in our midst in this material world. It also means that the promise of eternal life is not only for heaven but can be experienced even now.

A few years ago, the British relief organization Oxfam had a slogan that challenged the unfortunate tendency among Christians to speak of God's promise in only the future tense. "We believe in life before death," their signs proclaimed. Incarnation declares that what is coming to life *for* us may also come alive *in* us.

EMBODYING GOD'S COMMUNITY
ISAIAH 61:1-4, 8-11

William Faulkner, a great Southern writer of the last century, received his Nobel Prize for literature in 1950. It was an era when the world was captivated by the awesome technologies of destruction that had literally exploded onto the scene during the Second World War. Every decision was made in the shadow of the nuclear clouds that had obliterated Hiroshima and Nagasaki and which threatened the cities of the United States and the Soviet Union as the Cold War began in earnest. What stories were left to tell in a world that lived in fear of imminent annihilation?

Faulkner's acceptance speech was a reminder of why we value literature and why writers keep telling stories. Despite the frightening specter of atomic warfare, what was essential about the world had not changed. The qualities of humanity that make the world a livable place were still the qualities most needed. He said that a writer "must teach himself that the basest of all things is to be afraid: and, teaching himself that, forget it for-

ever, leaving no room in his workshop for anything but the old verities and truths of the heart, the universal truths lacking which any story is ephemeral and doomed—love and honor and pity and pride and compassion and sacrifice."[2]

We return to Isaiah once more in this third week of Advent. The collection of prophecies that bear this name is generally thought to derive from three distinct periods within the history of the nation of Judah.

In Chapter 61, we are hearing words meant for the first generation of those concerned with the restoration of Jerusalem after the exile in Babylon. As a people living in times of dislocation and fearful change, despair and uncertainty were creeping in. Old truths seemed to have vanished, and what lay ahead was difficult to contemplate. There was no assurance that things would come out well in the end. What did God have to say to them?

What the prophet set before them seemed impossible. Isaiah spoke of a future of blessing when old ruins would be rebuilt, when flocks and vineyards would flourish, and when their children would be known among the nations. The people were not just going home, but their true worth as the people of God's favor would be recognized.

Isaiah's vision is a communal one. It is rooted in a sense of God's justice and identity with those who had suffered. Just as God had spoken to Moses from a burning bush and said, "I have observed the misery of my people who are in Egypt. . . . I know their sufferings" (Exodus 3:7), God then spoke through the prophet to proclaim a new day for the oppressed, the broken, the captive, and the mourning. Just as in that previous experience of liberation from slavery, so God promised an upheaval of the powers that be and a reordering of society so that God's intentions can be made known.

Verses 5-7, omitted in today's reading, suggest a tone of revenge in the reversal of fortune for the people of Jerusalem. God's people had been laboring in a foreign land to build up the nation of Babylon. In the restored kingdom, strangers will watch *their* flocks and foreigners will till the land. The wealth of the nations will flow to Jerusalem. The aggrieved will always imagine a day when their restoration corresponds with the humiliation of their oppressors; but in Isaiah's vision, the point is not revenge but the glory of God. God's favor and compassion is made evident. Old wrongs are righted. The people are planted and rooted in the land like oaks. They receive all of this so that God's glory will be seen.

In verse 8, God tells the people that "I will make an everlasting covenant with them." In doing this, the God of Israel was simply going back to the earliest days of the relationship. As God called Abram out from an eastern land to go west to what would become the people's Promised Land, the Lord made a covenant. In it, God pledged to bless Abram and Sarai (later renamed Abraham and Sarah) with land and descendants.

However, the covenant, even then, included an implicit blessing for the nations (Genesis 12:1-3). God's relationship with their family and with the nation of Israel that followed was to be a visible sign of God's presence in the world. Other nations would be able to see in this relationship the in-breaking of a new reality and, ultimately, blessing for themselves.

God's becoming present in the physical stuff of the world is called *incarnation*. We associate this word with Jesus, the Word made flesh, and we talk about the unique way that God became human in him. However, a kind of incarnation was at work in the people of Israel, too. Israel, through its sufferings and in its struggles to be a sign of the living God in the material world, embodied its faith. When it lived out of a vision of God's justice, it revealed God, even in the midst of the most bleak and helpless situations, coming into the world.

When I was a child, I felt fortunate to grow up in a small town in rural Virginia. My father worked on the town's Main Street, as did the father of my friend Philip Jaderborg. The two of us spent many hours whiling away the time after school, treating the town as our playground until our fathers could take us home. We scrounged to buy baseball cards at the convenience store, walked along the railroad tracks that ran through the center of town, and rattled the knobs on the archaic vending machine at the laundromat to see if any free snacks would fall. I even remember sneaking into the upper level of the furniture store to take naps when I was not feeling well. Wherever we went, though, there were people who knew us and looked after us, even disciplined us, because they were part of organizations that put them into relationship with our families.

I am sure that many people felt insecure in that place. Racial tensions especially were no stranger to our hometown. However, I was always grateful to have known a community that provided me a matrix from which to grow. The presence of these people who knew me reminded me that I was not alone in the world. I was part of something bigger, with relationships and responsibilities into which I was growing.

Later I was challenged by my church to take on some of that role with members of the community who were intellectually challenged. That experience transformed my sense of vocation.

So to what does God call the people to in Isaiah 61? Is it merely freedom and the opportunity to lord it over their oppressors? Or is Isaiah's vision a call to a different sort of community in which God's justice is realized? It is a call to a land where those who have been broken and abused can find wholeness and healing. It is a call to see God's favor coming, not just to the healthy, the strong, and the well-placed, but to those who are living on the edge. It is a call to give up our fascination with the terrors of the world and to rediscover those things that make us human. As Faulkner said, "Love and honor and pity and pride and compassion and sacrifice."[3] In this way, we give glory to God.

These words do not remain in ancient history with the exiles. They are lifted up again as Jesus read them in his hometown synagogue and began his public ministry (Luke 4:18-19). They ring out centuries later, whenever we are confronted with a world that seems to be captivated by horror and impervious to change. They haunt this season of Advent as only the Spirit of the Lord can do, awaiting embodiment and incarnation in the people of God.

When have you felt yourself to be part of a community that embodies Isaiah's vision? How do fear or despair prevent you from being a blessing to others to the glory of God?

DON'T WORRY, BUT DON'T JUST BE HAPPY
1 THESSALONIANS 5:16-24

If the Spirit of the Lord was upon Isaiah, anointing him for mission in the world, the concern of Paul in writing to the Thessalonian Christians was that they not quench that Spirit (1 Thessalonians 5:19). Formed by the Spirit that was in Jesus, they were living in expectation of Christ's return; and they were getting antsy. Questions had started to arise. When will that return be? What if we die before he gets here? How can we be assured of our ultimate fate?

Christians through the generations have raised the same questions. Some within Christianity believe that the most important thing for the church to be concerned about is what happens to us after death.

A church sign down the road from me once read, "Your future depends on what you do in the present." However, the sign was not fully accurate. Christian life also embraces the present at the same time that it looks to the future. The present and the future are in question.

God will come again in Christ to bring to fulfillment the process of reconciliation. Our anxiety about our fate is not going to change that, but how we live in the world while we await that future is a sign of what we believe about what God is up to in the present. Paul invites us to rejoice, to pray, and to give thanks (verses 16-18).

One of my early jobs was as a part-time country-music disc jockey. During this time, I discovered the "hurts so good" song. Some days when I felt especially heartsick, I would go to the house I shared with my roommates, go

into my room, and throw a George Jones record on the turntable. (For those too young to remember such things, a record was like a vinyl MP3 file that you kept in a cardboard sleeve. Very primitive.) The needle would etch itself down in the groove of the record, and George would sing, "He stopped loving her today" or some other tale of lost love and woe. It felt like George knew exactly what I was feeling, and the needle was settling right into my soul to pick up every note.

The experience of traveling those emotional journeys in song with country singers helps me understand what it means to talk about joy in the context of real life. Being happy is not the same thing as rejoicing. Being happy is an emotion. Rejoicing is about knowing that our hope, our promise, and our life are in God, who comes to us in Jesus. It is also about desiring God's good for others as well as for ourselves. So no matter what our present circumstances, we have within us the capacity to see the world in the light of God's presence within us and among us. This capacity leads to what Paul understood as *joy*. *To rejoice* is to live with and to share this joy with one another.

In a recent book entitled *Against Happiness*, Eric Wilson combats what he sees as the culture of happiness that has grown up in the United States. Wilson does not begrudge the feeling; but he worries that we have replaced some deeper, more difficult emotions with an emphasis on being shiny, happy people. He notes "a collective yearning for complete happiness" and says that if we cannot achieve that state that we will medicate ourselves to get it. "If we can only be happy, are we merely trying to slice away what is probably an essential part of our hearts, that part that can reconcile us to facts, no matter how harsh, and that also can inspire us to imagine new and most creative ways to engage with the world?"[4]

Sometimes churches become hard places to share the "not so happy" parts of our experience, particularly in this season of the year. Out of a misunderstanding of Paul's command to "rejoice always," they may unintentionally be saying that there is no room at the inn for the blues.

United Methodist pastor Ann Robertson tells the story of a personal friend who was going through a difficult period in her life. She had a son in prison, another on the verge of a breakdown, a husband in the hospital, and she herself was depressed. "She never told a soul in her church and expended all of her energy putting on this cheery front at work because she thought that to reveal her depression would be a bad witness for her faith."

Robertson concludes that our definitions are skewed. "Happiness," she says, "is the great feeling that you get when everything is going smoothly. Joy is what God gives you in the midst of trouble when you put that trouble in God's hands."[5] God is in the midst of joy; and joy is knowing, even in the depths, that God's new day is coming. Joy also inhabits our appreciation of the incredible immensity of God's love for the world in the present instance.

One drab December day, in the midst of the Christmas blitz, I was rushing about my normal routine, heedless of any wonder. I drove to the intersection of a small road with the main highway. I looked left to check oncoming traffic, and then I turned right. There, just above the gas pumps of a grimy convenience store, was a brilliant moon. Surely that moon had never been in the sky before. It was huge and orange; and why every car on the road did not stop to consider it, I do not know. The whole character of the universe changed when I looked at that moon. It was joy—entirely unexpected and out of all proportion to the circumstances.

Theologian Karl Barth said, "Joy is really the simplest form of gratitude."[6] It is the thanks our soul gives to God when it is aware that life is a gift. So the joy and the prayer and the gratitude that Paul talks about come together in this realization.

Each of Paul's instructions in verses 16-18 has a similar difficult qualifier. Rejoice *always*. Pray *without ceasing*. Give thanks *in all circumstances*. It is this unceasing quality of the actions that leads me to believe that we must be made in such a way that our souls are meant to "rejoice in God [our] Savior," to quote Jesus' mother, Mary (Luke 1:47). If we had not been so dehumanized by the terrors of the world we might know that more fully. Rejoicing, praying, giving thanks—these are the things our souls do in their natural state. It takes an effort to close ourselves off to them; but when we allow the cares of the world to overwhelm us, then we can miss them.

Paul's concern in writing to the Thessalonians, a community anxious about what would happen to them in the future, seems to be to point them toward being human in the here and now. The admonitions to do these things without ceasing may have just been a way to say, "Remember who you are. Remember who Jesus was. Remember that he was God become human. Remember that you can become what God made you to be, truly human, because of Jesus. Rejoice always because you live in the light of what God has done in Jesus."

Have you experienced a deep sense of joy in spite of difficult circumstances? When? What was it like? What does the experience say to you about God? about yourself?

IN PRAISE OF SIGNPOSTS
JOHN 1:6-8, 19-28

Let us go back to the wilderness with John. In Mark's Gospel, we hear about John's ministry and the way he looked and where he lived. In the Gospel of John, we hear about who John was; or maybe it is better to say that we hear who John was not. John was at the center of a debate over his identity.

As we noted in last week's study, John fit the image of a classic prophet. His burden, like that of the prophets of old, was to hold the world up to the harsh light of God's judgment and say, "God expects more from you." There were many people who began to believe that John was not only a prophet, but that he might have been "the prophet" or a prophet who fulfilled messianic expectations (verse 21).

Maybe John was the one Israel had been waiting on. Maybe John was the Messiah or a second Elijah, the greatest of the prophets of old. The Jewish leaders from Jerusalem sent representatives to the wilderness to interrogate John. They asked, "Who are you?" John simply answered that he was not any of the people they suspected him of being.

The questioners continued: "Let us have an answer for those who sent us. What do you say about yourself?" (verse 22). John answered in a mysterious way. He claimed the role of witness by quoting Isaiah 40:3: "I am the voice of one crying out in the wilderness, / 'Make straight the way of the Lord,'" In contemporary terms, John was saying, "I am the precursor, the advance agent, the herald.

But you shouldn't worry about me. I'm not the main event."

Then he said, "Among you stands one whom you do not know" (verse 26). The statement suggests that they may have been preoccupied with people who seemed to threaten the existing way of life. John said of the one among them, the one who would come after him, "I am not worthy to untie the thong of his sandal" (verse 27).

John's world is not so far removed from our own. Advent comes with the deep sense that not all things are as they should be. Perhaps that is why Jesus used the image of a thief in the night to describe his coming again (Matthew 24:42-43; Luke 12:39-40).

When we are unaware, Jesus slips up on us to interrupt the comfortable ways we conspire with the world to forget about God's radical message of transformation. When we lose the language and the capacity to talk about what God expects of us and how God can change us, the holy, living God has to interrupt the world as we know it.

We are forgetful. We have to remind ourselves of what our baptisms mean. We can get run down by the world or run over by the world. We give service to Jesus with our lips but deny him with our actions. We can believe that bills or lost loves or job disappointments or even grief are the most serious threats to our lives. Our minds wander, and our focus fades. For this sort of people the God of life has to come as an interruption. We need a message that tells us God is not through with us yet.

Once again it is a call to incarnation. We are called to be the Christmas we are waiting for. The world will try to co-opt this *holy day* and make it merely a *holiday*. The world will try to take away its threatening character and repackage Christmas solely as sweetness and light. The world will domesticate Christmas, but it needs to hear something more from the people who know what it is all about.

We hear endless debates in this season about how the culture is at war with the church and about how seldom the true meaning of Christmas is expressed in the things we see in the shopping malls and on our television screens. It is true that the culture, for whatever reasons, some of them noble, has downplayed Christmas and made it into merely a secular winter festival. However, if there is a cultural war on Christmas, I say that we refuse to fight it.

What does the culture need to hear from Christians this Christmas? It does not need to hear an assertion of Christian rights; it needs to hear and see and experience a witness to whom this Baby in a manger is. Stores cannot be surrogates for the work that Christians are called to do. If a store decides to drop references to Christmas in their advertising, perhaps that is for the best because that store is not a community intent on living out the good news of Christ. The church is that community. Stores will sell the world the trappings of a holiday that they cannot faithfully proclaim. Only the church can do that. Only people who have had their lives turned upside down by the God who comes to a manger can faithfully proclaim and live out this message.

Who will tell the story? Who will share the word? Us? We seem an unlikely lot. We are no better than the next, but we can be the sort of signpost that John became. We can point the way. We can incarnate the message of Jesus in the world. We not only need to be the Christmas we are waiting for, we get to be the Christmas we are waiting for.

What preoccupations threaten to distract you from what is essential about this season? How are you pointing the way to the coming Christ?

[1] From *God Is in the Manger: Reflections on Advent and Christmas*, by Dietrich Bonhoeffer, edited by Jana Reiss (Westminster John Knox Press, 2010); page 52.
[2] From William Faulkner's Nobel Prize acceptance speech (December 10, 1950); *rjgeib.com/thoughts/faulkner/faulkner.html*.
[3] From William Faulkner's Nobel Prize acceptance speech.
[4] From "The Happiness Addicts Missing Out on a Melancholy Miracle," by Eric G. Wilson at TheAge.com (March 1, 2008) *theage.com.au/news/in-depth/the-happiness-addicts-missing-out-on-a-melancholy-miracle/2008/02/29/1204226981533.html*.
[5] From the sermon "Joy or Happiness?" by the Reverend Anne Robertson, delivered at St. John's United Methodist Church (1999); *stjohnsdover.org/99adv3.html*.
[6] From *Church Dogmatics*, III.4, by Karl Barth (T. & T. Clark, 1961); page 376.

Making Space for God

Perhaps your house is like mine—it is accumulating stuff. Do you see how I did not take any responsibility for it? *The house* is accumulating stuff, as if I had nothing to do with it; but, of course, I did. I have been bringing stuff into my house for years and not taking nearly enough out. The late comedian George Carlin once had a routine in which he described a house as "just a pile of stuff with a cover on it." In his absurd, reductionist style, he noted, "If you didn't have so much stuff, you wouldn't need a house. You could just walk around all the time."[1]

The real problem with stuff, though, is not that we do not have the freedom to walk around but that we do not have the space in which to welcome God. The material objects in my home are symptomatic of something similar going on in my soul. There are so many ways that I fill my life with unnecessary things that I often fail to make room for what is essential. I do not allow God to enter in and do the heavy cleaning that needs to be done.

Christmas draws ever closer. Perhaps we are aware of how much of our time is being dedicated to getting "stuff" bought or ready. How are we doing in challenging the messages our culture is sending about stuff? Do we trust the gospel message that our hope is not in what we can buy?

In the Scriptures for this week, the Gospel passage is taking center stage. Whereas in the first weeks of Advent, the Gospel passages looked back to the Old Testament promises; now the Old Testament passage is clearly being read in light of the Gospel. Even so, the story of David's desire to create a house for God stands out. In Romans, Paul's letter concludes with a dramatic statement of the importance of God's revelation in Jesus. In Luke, we encounter Mary who, in her very body, made space for the God who comes among us.

WHAT SORT OF HOUSE DOES
GOD REQUIRE?
2 SAMUEL 7:1-11, 16

Even for the great King David, God was sometimes an afterthought. The shepherd boy who became the most renowned of Israel's rulers was capable of singing psalms of praise and dancing with holy joy, as when he led a grand procession bringing the ark of the covenant into Jerusalem (2 Samuel 6:12-14). He was, the Scriptures say, a man after God's own heart (1 Samuel 13:14). Despite his reputation, however, David could be shockingly heedless of God's desires.

In one particularly bad stretch, just four chapters further along from our reading, David managed to mangle a majority of the Ten Commandments. In the course of a few months, David slept with another man's wife; arranged the man's murder; and had the audacity to get worked up over the injustice of it all when his court prophet, Nathan, presented the situation to him in the form of a parable. It was only when Nathan pointed the accusing finger at him with the words "You are the man" that David realized the depths of his sin (2 Samuel 12:7).

In this earlier episode, we find David settling in Jerusalem, the new capital he had established for the people of Israel. Ensconced in a palace made of cedar with his enemies subdued and his power unchallenged, David realized that there was something missing. There was no place for God. The ark, which had accompanied the people in their wilderness journey to the Promised Land, still looked as if it were decked out for the desert. It was still surrounded by portable curtains. Surely it required a more appropriate house, something more permanent. So David set out to make amends for the oversight and perhaps for the bad public relations. How did it look for a nation that supposedly had God as its ultimate authority to have a tent as the seat of that authority?

God, however, had a different understanding of what sort of space needed to have been created. Despite David's tendency toward God-forgetfulness, God had made a stand with this sometimes-wayward king and with the often-wayward people.

When Nathan received a divine word to share with the king, it was a restatement of the covenant God had made with Israel since the beginning. For no evident reason, certainly not because of any merit on their part, God had taken up residence among this people. A tent was as appropriate a dwelling as any for this deity. God was not demanding a house of cedar like David's. God desired a people who would show the divine presence in the world.

In the end, God turned the tables on David. David wanted to build a house for God, but God wanted to build a house for David. The house would not be a palace. The comfortable dwelling David had built would not last. Like Jerusalem itself, it would fall and crumble. However, God promised a house that would be a sign of enduring hope. A descendant would come who would make God's name visible in the world; and though kingdoms may rise and fall, the relationship between David's house and God would not end.

We cannot help reading these words in the light of Christmas. We are supposed to read them that way during this time of year. The Gospel reading makes a point of telling us that the angel Gabriel came to a young woman betrothed to a man named Joseph "from the house of David" (Luke 1:27). Suddenly a new story broke out. David's kingdom may have been just a memory, political vassals of Rome may have occupied the palace, but God had not forgotten the house of David. Jesus would be the embodiment of that promise uttered long ago.

Like David, I long for a space for God. The longing may be an afterthought. It may strike me as a moment of discomfort in my otherwise comfortable world. It may be a sense that perhaps I should have been more aware of God in the midst of my day. I should have prayed. I should have been paying attention. Perhaps, like David, I respond by wanting to make a grand gesture in the external world to make up for the lack I feel within.

At such times, I need an Advent friend like Nathan who can be that external expression of God's presence to me. Why does Nathan represent Advent? Nathan had the capacity to remind David of who he was, even to call him to confession. Nathan recalled and renewed God's promises. Nathan reminded David that whether he waited on God a lot or a little, God was waiting on him.

Fortunately God does not wait for us to be ready before entering the world. The Temple did not have to be built for God to be among the people. A room did not have to be vacant at the inn. All of our preparations and gestures toward God are always insufficient and untimely. However, along with David, we always walk into a story that began long before we arrived. We bear on us and in us the mark of our Maker, who has claimed us and who dwells in the world before we ever have eyes to see.

The space to welcome Jesus Emmanuel is ours from birth. It is clouded over by sin and by the many cares of our hearts in a broken world, but for all that the space is not lost. We can still enter that space of communion with God. In the wise words of a friend, in a moment of light on an otherwise dark day, in the embrace of a child, in a desperate prayer, we can be open to God.

Psalm 51, which is attributed to David following his sin with

Bathsheba, is a prayer for God to renew the deepest parts of our souls. "You desire truth in the inward being," the psalmist says. "Teach me wisdom in my secret heart" (verse 6). A temple may be a fine expression of God taking up residence on earth, but God already has a home. It is within us, waiting to be renewed.

In what ways has God become an afterthought in your life? What areas of your life are you closing off to God's presence? How might you find space to become aware of God's presence?

WALKING INTO GOD'S STORY
ROMANS 16:25-27

The closing benediction from Paul's Letter to the Romans lifts up the God who reveals startling news. Ancient secrets had been revealed in Jesus Christ and in the words of the prophets. A word of life had broken out to all the earth; and in the light of that knowledge, nothing could ever be the same.

The reading from Second Samuel reminds us that God makes promises that endure. In that reading, Nathan's prophecy looked ahead to the time when a new king would arise in the line of David. Romans looks back to how Israel's history reaches a climax in the person of Jesus, who can now be seen as that new king. Old promises were coming to fruition. The course of history was being made clear.

All of the admonitions and theology that Paul had shared with the Roman Christians through the course of this letter are grounded on this summary conviction: that Jesus changes things in a definitive way.

William Faulkner famously said that, for Southerners, "the past is never dead. It's not even past."[2] Most of his writing came from his awareness that his native Mississippi was wrapped in narratives that determined how its inhabitants saw the world and, therefore, how they acted in it. Particularly in the mid-20th century, Southerners were coming to grips with the legacy of slavery, the impact of the American Civil War, and their place within the larger world. All of that came through in Faulkner's writing.

In my corner of the South, on the Eastern Shore of Virginia, there is a similar sense of the weight of history. Because this little peninsula has been so isolated from the rest of the country for most of its history, many people are able to trace deep family roots in this area. Since it was also one of the earliest areas of permanent European settlement in the Western Hemisphere, the Shore has also been a place for the confluence of native, African, and European peoples for about 400 years.

Even those of us who come from elsewhere to live here end up dealing with this complex past. In recent years, I have become part of a small group that gathers in the light of that history. We are of

European and African descent, some of us with ancestors or more immediate family who lived on the Shore. We get together because we enjoy one another but also because we recognize that the particular way that race relations have developed in our community demands healing action.

Divisions and inequities still fall dramatically along racial lines. All of the members of our small group are engaged in activities and organizations that are working to better the community; but we get together, in part, to explore what a new way of being together might look like.

Sometimes we gather at a home that dates back to the 18th century. It is a beautiful place with tall trees and a tidal creek opening out into the Chesapeake Bay. One winter night as we met together, the wind rattled the "bones" of this old house as we talked about the roots of contemporary problems plaguing our county. It was impossible not to hear the voices of those who had gone before in that wind.

Native peoples had fished these waters. English capital and African labor had helped to build that place. An American story was played out there; and if peace-building would come, it would be because a revelation had come to this generation. The way forward is with our eyes open and living in soulful communion with one another.

Once we know from whence we have come, our actions in the future should be different. That was Paul's insight as he addressed the Roman Christians. God had brought together unlikely people who shared a story. Some had been born into the story and the promises contained in the Scriptures of the Jews. Others had come to the story through the good news of Jesus. God had always intended it as good news for the whole world. That became inescapably clear in Jesus.

However we made it to this story, it has become our story. We are part of God's story. We are established, as the benediction says, so we live differently in the world. We come to the "obedience of faith" that leads to follow Jesus, not out of compulsion, but out of the knowledge that his coming has transformed our lives and our will. We do things differently than we did before.

Cardinal Emmanuel Suhard is credited with the saying that Christians are called "to live in such a way that one's life would not make sense if God did not exist."[3] We can live our lives that way. We can pay lip service to the notion that God is in the world but then act as if that is not true.

However, once God is in the manger, once the world is revealed as God-filled instead of God-forsaken, once God has come in Jesus, no space we inhabit can be the same. We are called to walk into God's story. We are given the opportunity to claim a new way of being in the world, one that is grounded in confidence that God will bring about a new reign, to which we are invited to say, with Paul, "Amen."

What things are you doing in your life as a result of your "obedience of faith"? Where is God calling you to walk into God's story and claim a new way of being in the world?

A CREATIVE COLLABORATION
LUKE 1:26-38

History is not the only thing that shapes life on the Eastern Shore. Geography plays its role as well. A chain of uninhabited barrier islands stretches down the Virginia coast, defining the landscape of one of the last undeveloped stretches of the Eastern seaboard. Behind those islands are broad bays and marshes that are fertile zones for all sorts of marine life. Kayaking across these bays, I am often surprised by the large fish and even seals that pass through these sheltered waters.

In my mind's eye, I imagine the land as an engaged partner with the waters. Those islands bow out, sometimes miles from the mainland, as if to create a nursery for life to spawn and flourish. Like a pregnant woman, the land is opening space within itself for things to be born—and they are. The waters teem with shining, scaly fish; toothsome sharks; gliding crabs; and undulating rays.

The story of Mary leads me to think this way about geography.

Our stories of her are so limited. Even here, where Mary is the center of the story as the angel Gabriel comes to tell her about Jesus' birth, she says little. "How can this be?" she asks in verse 34. "Here I am, the servant of the Lord; let it be with me according to your word," she assents in verse 38.

I always wish for a more fiery response to this outrageous news, a little more protest. After all, what the angel proposed as God's favor could have sounded like an impossible burden. She was only betrothed, not married. What would the neighbors think? What would Joseph think? How does one live up to being the mother of God's Son?

Mary could have refused. She could have argued with God, like Moses did, that someone else should be chosen for the task. Instead, she followed the model of Hannah, another unlikely mother from Israel's history. She saw what God was up to in the world. When she sang of God's work a few verses later (verses 46-55), Mary understood that what was happening in her was a reflection of God's upside-down kingdom where fortunes are reversed, the lowly are lifted up, and the lofty are leveled. Mary was able to say yes to God because she could see that it was not all about her. A much bigger narrative was playing itself out.

Hannah's story is an instructive parallel. First Samuel 1:1–2:10 presents the mores and customs of a long-gone culture as we read of Hannah's despair over her childlessness. She was one of two wives of an Israelite man, and the other wife had children. Tension over the situation led to division and dissension in the family.

Hannah went to the Temple to pray to God for a son, vowing that she would dedicate him to the Lord. When the long-sought child was born, Hannah sang a song that emphasized God's universal reign. Her joy was not solely for herself but for the world. God "raises up the poor from the dust" and "lifts the needy from the ash heap" (1 Samuel 2:8). God had come into this particular woman's life and by doing so had changed the world.

Mary eventually got to her song of a world upended by God's action, but she was surprisingly calm and receptive in her initial encounter with the angel. I think I want a more rebellious outcry from Mary because I fear for her independence. Maybe it is because of the language the angel used. When, in Luke 1:35, Gabriel said, "The Holy Spirit will come upon you, and the power of the Most High will overshadow you," it sounds like God was running roughshod over Mary's life. No one wants to be overshadowed, do they?

Mary heard something different, though. Her acceptance of the angel's message indicates that she was not concerned about losing her life. Her joy as she sang the song we know as the Magnificat says that she saw the story of her particular life as one that was caught up in a much bigger story. Her life was now part of God's salvation story for the whole world.

Early Christians recognized that Mary's role as a willing human agent for God's incarnation had importance for all humanity. In the eighth century, eastern Christians began singing the Great Canon of Saint Andrew, which calls upon Mary as the Holy *Theotokos,* or bearer of God. The prayer calls out: "Hail, Womb that held God! Hail, Throne of the Lord! Hail, Mother of our life!"

Commenting on the canon, Frederica Mathewes-Green notes that Mary, "by bearing Christ in her womb, represents the Burning Bush which bore God's fire; she is the mercy seat and the ark of the covenant; she is the throne of God. Her womb contained the Creator of all, making her body 'more spacious than the heavens.' as an ancient hymn says."[4]

The language of that ancient hymn is dramatic, and we might say overblown; but how else do we describe what was happening? That the One who made all things and who is beyond all things should be constricted to human form as a baby is hard enough to get our minds around. Why not imagine the cosmic transformation of Mary's body to accommodate such a mystery? Beyond Tabernacle or Temple, Mary showed how God could inhabit even human flesh.

The canon, which is still sung during Lent in Eastern Orthodox churches, has a deep awareness of what flawed vessels human beings are for carrying divine fire. Our lives are riddled with contradictions and fears, failures and flaws. Sin distorts the structures of society and our very souls. We do not even know ourselves. The appeal to Mary in the canon is made in the middle of pleas for mercy.

Paul was aware of the same contrast between holy God and fallible flesh when he wrote to the Corinthian Christians and reminded them that "we have this treasure in clay jars" (2 Corinthians 4:7). The emphasis is on clay jars because God's transforming power is the work on display; but the acknowledgement that we have this treasure of God's presence in our very bodies is astounding, too. We have this treasure in clay jars, but we have this treasure!

I have seen, far too often, the ways in which people I love have neglected this aspect of the Incarnation. Because God has come into humanity through Jesus in Mary, we have the capacity to be bearers of God's light; but we are so blind to that capacity that we come to despise who we are or to despair that we can ever change. I have certainly been there myself. We can also despair for the world, but the Advent God comes to bring transformation.

There is a miraculous interplay in this passage between God's irresistible work of salvation and God's choice to do that work through human lives, even through human freedom. The angel's words to Mary speak of the grand currents of God's purpose coursing through history. The Child will receive the throne of David (as promised in the passage from 2 Samuel). He will reign over the house of Jacob, who was one of the first to inherit the covenant promise. Yet all of this will happen through the assent of this one woman.

To borrow from the Beatles, Mother Mary will have to whisper words of wisdom: "Let it be." Jesus came through the (pro-)creative collaboration of the Spirit present at the dawn of creation and a young girl in Palestine, probably no more than a teenager.

So much goes on in the week before Christmas as we struggle to tie up all the loose ends. Sometimes it seems that when the day finally comes, it will be more of an achievement than a celebration. However, this encounter of divine and human in the angel's visit to Mary is not about accomplishment at all. It is about receiving God and making room for Jesus to come. It is about seeing God's presence in the world around us and the ultimate victory of God's promises.

When the angel appeared, his opening words to Mary were "Greetings, favored one! The Lord is with you!" (Luke 1:28). He did not say that God "would be" with her or "had been" with her. The statement was in the present tense. It would take the birth of a savior for the world to know what Mary saw first. God has not forgotten the covenant. God is with us.

Why do you think Mary has been such an important figure for Christians through the centuries? What aspects of her story help you hear God's intentions for you?

[1]From "Stuff" From the 1986 *Comic Relief* (*babyboomerflashback.blogspot.com/2008/04/george-carlin-on-stuff.html*).

[2]From *Requiem for a Nun*, Act I, Scene III, by William Faulkner (Random House, 1951) *mcsr.olemiss.edu/~egjbp/faulkner/quotes.html.*

[3]From Cardinal Emmanuel Suhard (*cambridgestudycenter.com/quotesMindCulture.html*).

[4]From *First Fruits of Prayer: A Forty-Day Journey Through the Canon of St. Andrew*, by Frederica Mathewes-Green (Paraclete Press, 2006); e-book location 1030-1080.

Who Is That Unmasked Man?

Scriptures for Christmas Day:
Isaiah 52:7-10
Hebrews 1:1-12
John 1:1-14

Have you ever wondered why superheroes wear masks? A lot of the tension in comic book plotlines and the movies made from them comes from the tension of protecting a real identity and keeping it distinct from a hero persona. The superhero characters know that their lives would be irrevocably changed if word got out about their superpowers.

Contrast that with the way Jesus entered the world. He came on the scene in total vulnerability. He did not shield himself from the world but offered himself to it. He was the unmasked man who finally revealed the heart and purpose of God in fullness. He opened himself to rejection and ultimately was killed on a criminal's cross, but he was also visible and present and welcomed the world to discover its true identity as it received him. Jesus invites us to be unmasked people as well.

The Christmas Day readings open up the floodgates to unhindered joy. The period of waiting and watching finds its object in Jesus, but these readings also explore who this Jesus is. Unlike the Christmas Eve Gospel text from Luke that tells the *how* of Christmas, these texts want to talk about the *why*. Isaiah anticipates the joy by celebrating the cry of a messenger bringing good news to a ruined city. Hebrews lifts up Jesus with a host of titles explaining who he is. John ties the story together from Creation to birth by explaining that Christ has been present from the beginning.

The readings contain celebration, and they contain an invitation and a little bit of challenge. If we are tempted to think of Christmas as a holiday without consequences, we should stand convicted. Jesus comes to change things. This is good news for a lost and hurting world, but it also asks something from us. Jesus will transform us, and transformation is not always comfortable. However, if we see the world with Christmas eyes, we can perhaps see how—even in the here and now—God's reign is making all things new.

UNLIKELY BEAUTY
ISAIAH 52:7-10

Once I found myself stranded in a seaside marsh. I was kayaking back to the mainland from one of the barrier islands, and I used a narrow gut through the marsh to avoid the wind on the open water. It was the same passage I had used to go to the island, but I had not accounted for the change in water level at low tide. Water was draining out of the gut rapidly during my transit. Soon there was barely six inches of water to float my boat. Then there was none.

Salt marshes are fascinating places. They protect the land from the brunt of storms. They nurture marine life. They attract thousands of migratory birds that feed on their riches. They have a distinctive smell that I have grown to appreciate, if not enjoy. However, the prospect of spending several hours in the midst of one waiting for the water to rise was not appealing.

I was new to the area then. I did not understand the topography of marshes. I assumed I could just get out of my kayak and walk the boat forward to the next navigable spot. Wrong. When I stepped out, my right leg sank hip-deep in the marsh mud. Fortunately I had not committed the rest of my body; and I was able to haul my muddy self back into the kayak. I then spent several minutes jamming my paddle into the unstable soil and managed to pole the kayak forward inch by inch until I reached some water.

The rest of the trip was uneventful, but I carried a lot of mud back with me. The mud is the source of that unmistakable marsh smell. It is made up of dead plants and animals decomposing under the pressure of the water. It is a dark black; and it is difficult to wash off of your skin, often leaving a blue tinge. Once you know what it is, however, you realize that the mud is the most miraculous part of those fertile marshes. It is where dead things go to be reborn, so Eastern Shore people have claimed it. When someone comes and falls in love with this area, or when someone leaves and cannot get it off her mind, that one is said to have "marsh mud between their toes."

Beauty, the old saying goes, is in the eye of the beholder. I had to look at my muddy foot through the eyes of an ecologist to see the beauty. The prophet in this reading speaks of beautiful feet, too. "How beautiful upon the mountains / are the feet of the messenger who announces peace" (verse 7). It might have been difficult for Jerusalem to see that beauty. The city still lay in ruins. Days of glory were still the stuff of history; but for those with eyes to see, a new day was dawning.

Like architects who can look at an empty plot of ground and see a grand building, or visionaries who can look at a failed project and see opportunities for a new beginning, the prophet saw God coming to save the people. For him it was as self-evident as the sun: "In plain sight they see the return of the LORD to Zion" (verse 8). Let this singing begin! Let the word go out so that all the world will know! The promise of comfort, which we read about in Chapter 40, was being fulfilled (verse 9).

Because this is not the end of Israel's story we know that more dark days were ahead. The world was still a challenging place for God's people. Jerusalem would never again attain the independent status it had once held. However, the return from exile allowed the people to see that they had not been abandoned. God was still at work, and they had not been forgotten. For a people who could have fallen into hopelessness and despair, it was beautiful.

On Christmas Day, we read this passage in the light of another beautiful event that might have been difficult to see. God's advent, long-awaited, had arrived in the form of a baby. Born and placed in a manger, visited by shepherds who had their own distinctive smell, arriving outside the comforts of a house or inn, Jesus made an unlikely savior. Our Christmas pageants and stories of angels and brilliant stars make it seem that no one could have missed the message in this birth, but the whole story tells us that it was not inevitable that anyone would see what God was up to. It took the eyes of faith to know who Jesus was.

There is an old legend that on Christmas Eve, as midnight comes, the animals of the earth begin to speak and to tell the story of Jesus' birth. In our house, on that night, I sometimes look at Whiskers, our cat, and find myself wondering what she would say. It is exciting to think she may have a secret insight.

I have never heard Whiskers talk, though, nor any other animal, for that matter. Christmas dawns do not look any different from other dawns. The world still wakes to wars and woes, sorrows and trials; but a candle glowing at a midnight service says something beautiful is here. A word of hope in a Christmas carol says this Child Jesus is not going to let the world stay in bondage to its problems. A ringing bell in a church steeple says, "Your God reigns!" (verse 7). Do not be fooled by mud or gray skies or winter chill. The feet of God's messenger are beautiful.

What unlikely thing do you find beautiful? Why? Using your Isaiah eyes, what areas of your life or the world around you can you imagine as transformed by God's presence?

THIS CHANGES EVERYTHING
HEBREWS 1:1-12

Every family has them. Sometimes we are them. Eccentrics. People who walk to a slightly different beat. My family has its share. I had an uncle that everyone in the family wanted to name William Nicholas Alexander Amber Robert Thomas David Jingling Poker Fiddlestick Stumptoe Kitchen. We called him Uncle Nick. But if Uncle Nick got the eccentric name, Uncle Jim got the eccentric trophy.

Uncle Jim was a preacher and a teacher, among other things. By the time I got to know him, though, he was retired and living in a house on one of the main streets of a small Virginia town. He was well-known to the neighborhood because he would sit on the front porch of the house and greet people passing by on the sidewalk. He had a long, snow-white beard stained by tobacco. He was a bit unkempt, which befitted an old preacher living on his own.

Inside his house was a maze of old books and papers stacked floor to ceiling with a narrow path through them. It was a good representation of what his mind was like, too—a treasure trove of stories and biblical reflections and family history, all strewn about in no particular order. As a child, I sought out Uncle Jim at family reunions for exactly that reason; but I do not think many people

knew how to take him, and not many of my family members would have chosen him to be our representative to the rest of the world.

I get the feeling that the Christian family is not sure what to say about Jesus either. We are comfortable with Jesus being the great teacher who welcomed children and told wonderful parables. We like what he did with the disciples and the way he tweaked the sanctimonious religious leaders for their hypocrisy.

When we make exalted claims for who Jesus is, however, when we talk about him as someone who was more than just a human being who lived 2,000 years ago as the Son of God, it can make us nervous. This Jesus starts to make a claim on us and on the world. To believe in this Jesus is not to simply admire a great person from the past; to believe in this Jesus means to change and to be different and to be transformed. Do we want to change?

The Book of Hebrews will not let us get away with a Jesus who is not divine. Jesus may have been modest in his claims about himself in the first Gospels. He may have told people who knew who he was that they should not tell anyone else. He may have treated his identity as a secret at times, but the Christian community that followed Jesus could not say that. After walking through the death and the Resurrection, they knew that Jesus was more than another figure on the scene of history. Jesus was the one for whom all Israel had been waiting. Jesus was the one the whole earth had desired.

Hebrews uses exalted language to describe Jesus. It starts out with the note that in former times God spoke to us through the prophets, and the people of Israel could name them: Elijah, Isaiah, and Jeremiah. They had all tried to bring a word from God to tell the people that God had not forgotten the covenant with Israel and that a new day was coming. Now, however, God had spoken in a new way—through a son.

The author of this passage piled on the titles to make it abundantly clear that Jesus Christ was different. He is the appointed heir of all things. He is the one through whom God made creation. At the beginning of all things, Christ was there and everything was being made through him. This is the same thing John lifted up in the Gospel passage for today. We may have seen God in a new way in Jesus, but he was there at the beginning.

"He is the reflection of God's glory and the exact imprint of God's very being" (verse 3). Christ is the exact representation of God's essential nature, the one who most fully reveals God. Christ sits at the right hand of God, above even the angels. These are incredible titles to place on the figure of Jesus of Nazareth. They point to someone so unique that the only proper response is worship and praise.

Christ is at the center of what our life in the church is all about. Yet we can and do live as if Christ is not so central. If it is true that we cannot believe in a Jesus with such exalted titles without changing, then maybe the possibility of change is our biggest stumbling block. Perhaps we despair that we have the power to change. We cannot even change ourselves, much less this messy world that we live in.

At times we might find ourselves trapped in personal disasters where our relationships and our jobs and our health all seem to be spinning out of control. We wonder where we will find the power to change, and we certainly do not see what Christ has to do with it. If Jesus is just a man, then why worship him? On the other hand, if he is so exalted and raised up above us, who are we to him? We might say with the psalmist that is quoted in the next chapter, "What are human beings that you are mindful of them, / or mortals, that you care for them?" (Hebrews 2:6; Psalm 8:4).

Near the town of York in England, the monastic ruins of Fountains Abbey sit nestled in a small valley. The layout and some of the rooms of the abbey have survived. Near the dining hall, or refectory, is a huge fireplace, large enough to place a tree for burning. It was the only place in the entire abbey that was heated, and the monks were not allowed to be in this room except for a small portion of the day unless they were ill. This is a stone building, and northern England can be cold in the winter.

As I looked at that fireplace, I imagined a young monk entering the abbey and facing that first cold winter. I saw him in his rough wool habit, huddled by the stone wall separating him from that glowing fire, trying to soak up the little warmth that seeped through. I wondered what it must have been like for him trying to cope with the monastic schedule: waking up before dawn for worship, followed by study in the cloister and work in the gardens before a simple breakfast. How much did he wonder about the possessions and family he left had behind?

Yet in this new world, the monk encountered one figure in a dramatic way: Christ. The world of the monasteries, for all its flaws and limitations, was a Christ-shaped world that offered the power to change lives for those few who could take the vows and for those many who depended on the hospitality and service the monastics could provide. It was a place that challenged a world that struggled to believe that Christ could change things.

The influential Christian education professor Dick Murray used to say, "A high-tech world demands a high-touch Church." Christian community can be a "touching place" where the castoffs of a throwaway society can come to touch and be touched and to find the power to change. The church can be a different space, a unique space in a world that values style over substance. Christian communities can only be unique, however, if they believe that they are. They are unique because they see something healing for the whole world in Jesus Christ, who is all of those fantastic things that Hebrews says he is: representative of God and heir of all things.

However, as Jesus' incarnation shows, he is also one thing more. He is our brother who knows firsthand the lives we live and the deaths we die, who endured the suffering of crucifixion and death to show us that God is not just above us but also with us.

What would have to change in your life if you took seriously the claims of Hebrews about who Jesus is?

A GIFT FOR THE OPENING
JOHN 1:1-14

The Christmas story from the Gospel of Luke gives us the sensual data, the rough and gritty details of Jesus' birth in a manger in Bethlehem. When we read Luke, we hear the angels singing. We smell the sheep. We feel Mary's weariness. Maybe we even hear the Baby's cry. Luke gave us the narrow focus.

John wanted us to see something else. John wanted us to know that this story does not just begin with an angel visiting a young girl to tell her that she would be giving birth to a messiah. John knew that the story was greater than that. It was not just a baby like any other being born in that stable; it was God. The Creator of the universe had condescended to be found in human form. This Christ we know in Jesus was there at the beginning of all things. "In the beginning was the Word, and the Word was with God, and the Word was God." This Word is Christ.

John did not want his readers to forget the big picture. It is absolutely important that you know who this Jesus is. This was not just a great man who rose from humble birth to be a leader of his people. This was not a traditional hero's narrative. This was not just a Jewish leader or a great teacher. This was not just a prophet or even just a king. This was the one who was present at the creation—the one through whom all things have their being. Without this one not one thing was made. The whole universe has its origins in this one who is not only human but divine.

In *The Soul of Christianity*, Huston Smith, an author and scholar of religion, says that he has always thought of the Incarnation as a painful thing. It must be painful, he says, for God, who knows no limits of time and space, to be constrained to the form and time of a single human life. He recalls a time when he went to a Christmas Eve service after a hernia operation and heard the minister talking about God straining against the limitations of human existence, ready to burst out. Sud-denly, Smith says, his hernia operation was put into a new light.

It is astounding that God would choose to come in this way; and because God chose to come in this way, we almost missed it. Maybe we still do. John was fascinated by this. He said, "He was in the world, and the world came into being through him; yet the world did not know him. He came to what was his own, and his own people did not accept him" (verses 10-11). What if you gave a gift and no one knew it? What if people had the most amazing gift they could ever dream of right in front of them and they were absolutely blind to it?

When my son was young, he had a birthday party. There was nothing unusual in that. We had cake and played games, and friends and family brought gifts. What was different was that my son decided not to open the gifts. He just was not ready. So for two days after the party, the gifts sat waiting to be opened. It was not a source of anxiety for my son—only for his parents who were haunted by the unopened presents in the corner. We all celebrated when he decided the time was right, and he loved the gifts.

What if God's gift to us is like those presents waiting to be unwrapped? What if the miracle of the Incarnation is so close to us that we cannot even see it? To paraphrase St. Augustine, what if God is closer to us than we are to ourselves? So there is this amazing, incomparable gift that God has given us, promising us life and salvation. All that is missing is someone to open it up. All that is missing is us!

We need to show up for Christmas. This is the easy part because God already has done the hard work. God has done the painful work of taking on human form and entering our time and space, though God knows no such limitations. God has done the impossible in entering the world. All that is left is for us to open the present. We have been ripping the paper off of presents since infancy. We can get through the wrappings to find the toy beneath the tissue paper. Can we get through the wrappings to find God?

John started his Gospel this way for a reason. John did not want us to be content with hearing what God did. He wanted to move us to do something about it. It is not enough for us to know the details of the story of Jesus' birth. It is not enough to be awed at the angels and humbled by the shepherds. It is not enough to see the magi kneeling at Jesus' feet. It is not enough to feel for Mary and for Joseph and the trials they went through. It is not even enough to know that "the manger of Bethlehem cradles a king."

John wanted us to believe. John tells us right up front that the universe was made through this one. Each one of us was made through this one. Christ is the center point, the hinge on which the universe turns. Some will miss how important he is. Some will misunderstand. Some will have the gift right in front of them and not see what they have been given.

To those who believe, however, who received him and believed in his name, "he gave power to be children of God" (verse 12). It does not matter what we have been before or who we thought we were before. It does not matter if we are poor as a shepherd or rich as a king. It does not matter if we have walked the straight and narrow or fallen off the wagon. If we had to earn this gift, none of us would have done it; but if we receive this gift, then we can become what we were always meant to be: God's children.

There ought to be an extra figure in the Nativity sets we put up in our homes. Alongside the angels and shepherds, right there with the magi and the donkeys, right in there with the father and mother and baby Jesus, there ought to be a figure of you. If you are not part of this scene, if you do not see a place for yourself in God's family, then the Christmas story is just a nice old legend. However, John knows that it is so much more. It is about how God loves you and me and the whole world. That is a gift worth opening.

How has your journey through Advent this year helped you understand who Jesus is? What does it mean to you to have the power to become a child of God?